Dear Black Girl, You are IT!

A Guide to Becoming an
Intelligent & Triumphant Black Girl

PLEASE
DO NOT WRITE
IN THIS BOOK!

TAMERA ELYSE TRIMUEL

November Media Publishing, Chicago IL.
Copyright © 2020 *Tamera Elyse Trimuel*

marlene.trimuel@gmail.com

Ordering information: special discounts are available on quantity purchases by corporations, associations, and others. For details, contact the author at the email address above.

Printed in the United States of America
Produced by November Media Publishing & Consulting Firm

ISBN-13: 978-1-0878-7774-7

Contents

Special Thanks

I would like to give a special thanks to my parents, Terrence & Marlene Trimuel. Thanks for believing in me and encouraging me to grow beyond my fears and to share my gifts/talents with the world. Thanks for teaching me that God is my source for success and He will always direct my paths.

Thank you, Uncle Melvin Luckett, for choosing me to be the Brand Ambassador for your Intelligent & Triumphant brand, which inspired me to write this book!

Thanks to my Focus Group for believing in me and for all the crazy laughs and ideas you've contributed to my brand.

Thank you, November Media Publishing Company, for accepting me as a teen author and believing in my book and for bringing my vision to life.

You Are Free, Black Girl
By: Tamera Elyse Trimuel

You are Free, Black Girl, from all mishaps, negativity, and complacency.

You are Free, Black Girl, to discover your intelligence, your majesty, and from whom all your blessings flow.

You are Free, Black Girl, to discover your inner beauty and countless flaws.

You are Free, Black Girl, to offer no excuse for your greatness.

You are Free, Black Girl, to use your strength to give birth to a nation for love, hope, and prosperity.

You are Free, Black Girl, to uplift your black sister and pass the torch.

You are Free, Black Girl, to explore the endless possibilities to become a pioneer in your own life story.

You are Free, Black Girl, to create your own IT Flow so others can follow and create their own destiny.

You are Free, Black Girl, to create your own rhythm in life and dance to your own beat.

You are Free, Black Girl, to soar like an eagle to different levels in your life.

You are Free, Black Girl, to be ***Intelligent & Triumphant***

Introduction

Hey, Black Girl!

It's your girl, *Tamera Elyse Trimuel*. Thanks for joining me on this journey to show you how ***Intelligent & Triumphant*** you are as a Black Girl. I pray that you are ready, because I'm about to take you for the ride of your life!

I have created the Intelligent & Triumphant Flow Movement (*IT Flow Movement*) to show you who you are destined to become, because the world is trying to destroy your identity. We are an endangered species, and we must save ourselves before our true identity becomes extinct.

As a Black Girl, especially today, you have been systematically programmed not to appreciate and love yourself. However, God never created you to be ratchet, a video vixen, a side chick, promiscuous, sexually or mentally abused, and discounted by society. You are *Intelligent & Triumphant*, period! I am here to reverse how you view yourself. You may have been told you are less than perfect, or maybe you are not good enough; but Black Girl, **YOU ARE IT!** Allow me the opportunity to renew your mind so that you love the Black Girl you are purposed to become.

It is time for you to **STEP FORWARD** into your destiny and start to become your future *S.E.L.F.* Your future *S.E.L.F.* starts today with how you view yourself. How you see yourself today will determine your outcome in the future. When was the last time you talked to the girl in the mirror? Where do you see yourself in five years…10 years…or 20 years? Okay, maybe you aren't thinking that far in advance, but at least give it a thought. My book will inspire you to look beyond where you are now and help you to dream about your future *Intelligent & Triumphant* self.

To achieve greatness, you must first believe that you are not the clone that was created by reality TV! You are not superficial. You are a Black Girl who has morals and values—you deserve respect. You have virtues that must be treasured and appreciated by anyone you encounter. You are a Black Girl who is fearfully and wonderfully made with supernatural gifts and talents awaiting to meet the world. Go ahead and applaud yourself because you are about to introduce a new *S.E.L.F.* to the world. Allow me to be the first to congratulate you on becoming an *Intelligent & Triumphant* Black Girl! Now, let's discover who you are and how to become part of my amazing *IT Flow Movement*.

The IT Flow

Before you begin reading my book, let me tell you more about my *IT Flow Movement*. *IT Flow* stands for **Intelligent & Triumphant (IT) Free Lifestyle of Winning (Flow).**

- *IT Flow* is a movement where you create a daily routine of feeding yourS.E.L.F. with knowledge, wisdom, and understanding so you can be free to live the lifestyle of a winner. A winner is always triumphant and has a great impact on others.
- *IT Flow* is your own creative, unique way to encourage and inspire yourS.E.L.F. daily.
- *IT Flow* is your own private time to empower yourS.E.L.F.

You will begin your *IT Flow* each day by praying, playing music, jumping around, or whatever it takes to get your *IT Flow* going. Your *IT FLOW* will free and enhance your inner beauty. Your *IT FLOW* will help you to create a rhythm to showcase your intelligence and to dance in triumph like no one is watching.

My purpose for writing this book is to show you just how fabulous you are. Maybe you have heard this before, but just in case you haven't, I want you to know that you are ***Intelligent & Triumphant!*** Believing you are intelligent will make you triumphant in every area of your life. IT will make you think and flow like a winner. Winning is a lifestyle. ***I want you to stop looking at yourself as just ordinary, but as a Black Girl who has the power to transcend the barriers that are positioned to limit you.*** God gave you the strength, power, grace, and freedom to live your life in greatness.

God created strong examples of greatness to follow, like Maya Angelou, Michelle Obama, Oprah Winfrey, Serena Williams, and other phenomenal women. These women were created in His image, and they used their intelligence to overcome their obstacles and became triumphant history-makers. They are overcomers! If they could overcome the obstacles that were placed before them, why can't you? We set our own limits and live by them. I am asking you to get rid of your limits and step outside of your comfort zone. We are about to explore some new limitless rhythms that are going to give you a new beat to dance to. Don't be afraid to explore the unknown, because God has not given you a spirit of fear, but a spirit of love, power, and a sound mind!

Now, let's get started on creating your *IT Flow* so you can become an *Intelligent & Triumphant* Black Girl.

Chapter One

I Can Do All Things...

Be Inspired

I always thought of myself in a positive light, but something really clicked during my eighth-grade year. I was always confident, although I did have a few insecurities and moments where I questioned who I was because of the kids around me. For me, it started when I was in fourth grade, when I really began to struggle with my weight. I wasn't fat, but my shape wasn't like the other girls around me. I began to think, with the mind of a nine-year-old, that I had too much extra love on my body. I thought that I had to be a size zero to be considered acceptable to other people. I also became insecure about my clothes because I didn't have the latest fashion, the newest Jordans or Nikes. At that age, in my mind, you weren't cool if you didn't have those things.

My insecurity about my weight and how I looked in my clothes made me feel I wasn't cute and that other kids were laughing at me behind my back. I never cried or anything because I never wanted to show any signs of weakness, but deep inside, I was sad. Whenever my school would have dress-up day, the fear of not wearing my school uniform would trigger my insecurity of not having the latest fashion or shoes. As long as I was in my uniform, I was confident. As soon as dress-up day came, I was instantly insecure about the clothes I had to wear. I knew the other students would laugh at me because I did not have on name-brand clothes or shoes.

Fortunately, this was just a phase. I overcame those insecurities by understanding who I was and who I was meant to be. I finally understood that I wasn't meant to "fit in." I understood that the size of my body had nothing to do with the quality of my character. I understood that confidence is key and not to let the opinions of others dictate how I looked at myself in the mirror. I understood that it's not what you wear, but how you wear it. Honestly, maturity helped me overcome my insecurities.

I also began to repeat my two favorite affirmations in the mirror: "I am more than a conqueror" and

"I can do ALL things through Christ, who strengthens me." My brother and I had been taught these affirmations, which are Bible verses, by my parents, and I never stopped saying them, but sometimes I would forget what they meant and how powerful they really were.

In eighth grade, I hit a point of maturity that showed me who I really was, and I discovered why it is so important to hold my head high and to think of myself positively. I realized that I had the power of influence, which made me understand even more why it was necessary to think of myself as a princess and nothing less. I discovered that I had a gift and the only way I could share that gift with others was to share it with myself first. **I had to encourage myself before I could encourage anyone else.** And the only way to do this was to think of myself as a beautiful Black Girl who is destined for greatness.

Be Empowered

It is always good to have people around you that inspire & empower you! For me, my role models are my parents because they have shown me what true faith and resilience is. Also, they have been a tremendous support for me, and because of this I have been able to overcome a lot of my insecurities. My mother is the woman I aspire to be. I have seen her time after time deny her own personal desires, to care for her family. She is also a strong prayer warrior and has consistent visions and dreams. She always creates a way with God's guidance to reach her aspirations, and she has taught me how to be relentless in pursuing mine. My dad is a minister and a strong man of God. He always leads by example and has shown me how to use my voice to inspire others. He is very disciplined, and he has taught me that when you pray and are diligent in seeking God, He will provide. My parents have shown me what true sacrifice is and what it means to have unwavering faith.

Fortunately, I have been blessed to have parents who have poured endlessly into me and my dreams, and I feel that every young Black Girl deserves the same advantage, whether they receive it from a parent, family, friend or mentor. My parents have been encouraging me ever since I came out of the womb, and I see the importance of this now that I am older and encouraging others. Unfortunately, in this day and age, we don't have enough young black females in our age group acting in a way that most of us would like to reflect. I want to be one of the young Black Girls of my generation whom others look up to and are inspired by. I want young girls to understand that *"self-love is the best love and it is impossible to love someone else without fully loving yourself first."*

> "It's not who you are today, but who you will discover and inspire to become in your Mirror of Truth."

TAMERA ELYSE

Chapter Two

Fearfully and Wonderfully Made

Take the First Steps

Did you know that you are fearfully and wonderfully made by God? Did you know that you are smarter than you give yourself credit for? Did you know that you can accomplish anything that you put your mind to?

Well, if you didn't know, now you do! The *IT FLOW Movement* is where you will learn how to discover what it takes daily to achieve greatness. Black Girl, we were all created equal and with our own unique power. You must learn how to tap into the power within yourself to experience your greatness. *Your greatness begins with realizing that you are intelligent.* Being intelligent stems from tapping into your inner strength and power.

Your intelligence is an inside job. You were created by God in His image. God is beyond genius; what does that make you? A super-intelligent Black Girl!

I want to show you how to get into the flow of becoming the queen that you are. Let me show you how to begin each day in greatness. You will begin each day with affirmations that will empower you and allow your mind, body, and spirit to be aligned with God. This is crucial and must be done daily to stay in the *IT FLOW.* You must believe what you say. Are you ready? *Let's GO!*

STEP ONE:

I need you to find a mirror and make it your favorite. This mirror will become your *Mirror of Truth*. The Mirror of Truth will help you to discover the four areas of your *S.E.L.F.* The four areas will allow you to:

- *See* you.
- *Express* you.
- *Love* you.
- *Free* you.

Wow! I bet you never thought of looking at your **S.E.L.F.** in this way. It's okay because, once you are done reading my book, you will never look at your **S.E.L.F.** as just ordinary. The Mirror of Truth is where you will discover the real you and transform how you view your **S.E.L.F.**

To get into the IT Flow, you must begin each day with your Mirror of Truth. You have to be willing to empower and encourage yourself daily and stop depending on or expecting others to do it for you. This may take a lot of effort on your part because the only thing you normally use the mirror for is to see how you look and not to talk to yourself. But that's okay. Walk with me and trust me. You are about to have the time of your life talking and dancing with *your S.E.L.F.*

STEP TWO:

Ready? Let's begin your *IT Flow.* Look in the mirror. **Look at YOU.** You are the only person in the mirror. Can you see *IT?* Can you see the intelligence that God put inside of you? Remember, you were created in His image. You are super intelligent, and it is your time to *allow your intelligence to manifest.* Tell the person in the mirror the following:

Mirror of Truth Affirmations:

- I am *Intelligent & Triumphant.*
- I am fearfully and wonderfully made by God.
- I will start today to become my future *S.E.L.F.*
- I am a child of God.
- I am beautiful.
- I am educated.
- I am unique.
- I am extraordinary.
- I was created for greatness.
- I will encourage myself daily.
- I am more than a conqueror.

How do you feel? You should feel empowered! Your Mirror of Truth is designed not only to inspire you, but to help you to feel *Intelligent & Triumphant* in every area of your life. You are the only person who will appear in your Mirror of Truth. Strive to become stronger each day. Who you become depends on what you tell your *S.E.L.F.* daily. Don't compare yourself to others. Don't judge or criticize yourself too harshly. Learn how to love and empower your *S.E.L.F!*

As you continue reading, I will give you more affirmations. Repeat these affirmations daily to yourself in your Mirror of Truth. Your Mirror of Truth will change daily because you will begin to love yourself more than you did yesterday. Always remember to strive to become stronger each day, and don't judge or criticize yourself too harshly. Reward yourself and tell yourself every chance you get,

"Dear S.E.L.F.,
You are Intelligent & Triumphant
and I LOVE YOU!"

Mirror of Truth Reflection:

"It's not who you are today, but who you will discover
and inspire to become in your Mirror of Truth"
—Tamera Elyse

"Love is telling yourself
daily that your
imperfections were
created to make you
unique."

TAMERA ELYSE

Chapter Three

See You

"Who Is The Black Girl?"

Mirror of Truth Affirmations:

- I am strong.
- I am love.
- I am a girl with virtue.
- I will be an honor student.
- I will be a college graduate.
- I will be successful.
- I will embrace the melanin in my skin.

Now that you are in your *IT FLOW*, it is time to discover who the Black Girl is. The Black

Girl is a fearless, God-fearing, virtuous girl who is ready to show the world her God-given gifts and talents. *"**Black Girl, it is time for you to create your own music for your life and march to your own beat. It's your life, so you can design it any way you want.**"* Your life will be filled with ups and downs, but you got this! Remember, you are an *Intelligent & Triumphant* Black Girl, and you create the music you want to dance to.

Everything you need is inside of you. Try to see yourself through God's eyes since you were created in His image. Can you see your beauty, strength, and success? Can you see your bright future? The image you see in your Mirror of Truth is the image you will project to others. How do you want to *See You*? Well, the change starts with the affirmations you just told yourself. See yourself in the future as a successful Black Girl with an exciting career that will not only enhance your life, but will also have a great impact on serving others.

Look at the girl in the mirror. Really get a good look. Look beyond your flaws, imperfections, thickness, skinniness, acne, hair, and all the other girl issues. ***You have to let go of pain and negative images to see your beauty and intelligence.*** Can you start to see yourself? Can you see that you are enough, special, wonderful, exceptional, and beautiful? Can you see your *S.E.L.F* as the next doctor, author, film director, journalist, lawyer, nurse, engineer, or whatever your heart desires? Your virtue and morals are the building blocks that will create your inner beauty, which will shine through you and inspire others. Your future starts now! Start telling yourself that you need to put the work in now so you can dance in your triumph later.

Here's what you have to do:

Conquer your Fear

How are you fearless? I'm glad that you asked. First, you must remember who you belong to. Of course, you belong to your parents, but you also have a Heavenly Father who has created you for this exact time, place, and space. You were created with a specific purpose, specific gifts, and specific talents to be used to empower this world. You have no idea of the plans that God has for you, but He does: "'For I know the plans I have for you,' declares the LORD, 'plans to prosper you and not to harm you, plans to give you hope and a future'" (Jeremiah 29:11). You don't have to have all of the answers; you just need to trust the One who does.

You feel me? God's got you. There is no need to fear. Even when fear tries to creep in, shoot it down with your daily affirmations and girl power! Replace negativity with positivity. You have got to walk in the truth and knowledge of who God says you are. Psalm 139:14 says, "I praise you because I am fearfully and wonderfully made; your works are wonderful, I know that full well." Did you read the confidence in that scripture? That is the type of "God-fidence" you need.

Girl, look fear in the eyes and declare who you are and walk past it. I know it is easier said than done, but you can't let the girl in the mirror down. *What you do today is so important to becoming the woman you want to become in the future.* ***Let your intelligence manifest now and don't let fear get in your way!***

What are three fears that are constantly staring you in your face?

1. _____

2. _____

3. _____

How do you plan to kick fear to the curb and go after what you want?

_____

_____

_____

_____

_____

_____

_____

_____

_____

_____

_____

_____

Embrace the Black Queen:

Black Girl, you come from a lineage of women who changed history. Courage and bravery are the DNA within your veins. Your ancestors broke chains, abolished laws, fought for equal rights in the most inhumane of circumstances, and defied death. Yes, girl, defied death! You come from a race of women who used their voices no matter the cost to inspire and evoke change. Black Girl...you are of the highest royalty.

I know it may not seem like it at times, because society would have you to think that you are at the bottom of the barrel. They tell you to hate your brown skin and straighten your hair to rise to their level of beauty. Nope. You don't need to. You are perfect just as you are. Your skin is beautiful. Your hair is gorgeous. Black Girls are so awesome that the pigments of our skin tones can't be duplicated. No one color defines Black Girls. Isn't that amazing? It does not matter if your hair is not super straight. There is greatness wrapped in those curls, coils, and kinks. Look how Black Girls are embracing their natural hair and rocking those hairstyles. Black Girls were not created to be boxed in. Your level of beauty is beyond human comprehension. Your beauty can't be bottled up and sold. ***Black Girl, you have got to see how special you are! You are bold and creative. You are enough!***

Once you know the truth, you can live the truth, and it changes everything.

Give yourself a big HUG and say, "I See You. I see my Intelligence, and I Love You!

You Are a Virtue Girl

Black Girl, your virtue is valued far above rubies. As a Virtue Girl, you have to respect yourself first before others will. Being a Virtue Girl, with morals and values, helps to develop your character. You are a Black Girl with virtues. Let's check that definition so you can be clear on how important you are. The word "virtue" means "having or showing high moral standards." I want to share some words of wisdom from my parents. They taught me that:

1. A person respects what you respect.
2. You must show people how to respect you.
3. If you respect your morals and values, others will, too.
4. Don't lower your standards to meet another person's expectations.
5. If they want to be in your trusted inner circle, they will respect your morals and standards.

Black Girl, you are phenomenal! There is no reason for you to walk with your head down or feel shameful. *You have to let go of the pain and negative images to see your beauty and intelligence.* **You are excellent.** This does not mean perfection. You will make mistakes. You have probably made more than three already today. It's okay. Mistakes are lessons inside out. They do not define you. They are character-building tools. Mistakes do not take away from the goodness that is within YOU. God says that you are the head and not the tail. You are above and never beneath (Deuteronomy 28:13). You are God's chosen. If he approves of you, nothing else matters. Go ahead and let that Black Girl magic shine through.

Exercise:

List five mistakes that you regret. Next to each one, write out the lesson you learned, along with how it has built your character.

1. _____

_____

_____

2. _____

_____

_____

3. _____

_____

_____

4. _____

_____

_____

5. _____

_____

_____

_____

Look in your Mirror of Truth and say,

"Dear S.E.L.F.,
You are Intelligent & Triumphant, and I See
You as being a Black Girl of Greatness."

Mirror of Truth Reflection:

"Love is telling yourself daily that your
imperfections were created to make you unique."
—Tamera Elyse

Black Girl Journal Entry:

Write down what you see when you look at yourself. Then write down what you would really like to see when you look in the mirror. Don't be shy. Get real and get honest. Before you can reveal your intelligence and magic to others, you have to SEE IT and reveal IT to yourself first.

_____

_____

_____

_____

_____

_____

_____

_____

_____

_____

_____

_____

_____

_____

_____

Black Girl Prayer to See You

Heavenly Father,

Thank you for loving me unconditionally. Thank you for creating me with a purpose to do great things. Thank you for sending positive words to me when I feel down or that I am not good enough. Sometimes I feel like I am not the prettiest or the smartest, but you somehow send your love to remind me that I am everything that I should be. Help me to see myself the way that you see me. Help me to love myself more. Help me to not compare myself to others but to be okay in standing apart from everyone else. Help me to understand that those little quirky things are what make me unique. Show me the beautiful young woman that you said I am. Help me to embrace all that she is and to be patient with who I am, as I become her.

I love you, God.

Amen.

"Your Journey of Greatness begins when you open your Soul to Expression."

TAMERA ELYSE

Chapter Four

Express You

Unleash Your Greatness

Mirror of Truth Affirmations:

- I will let my light shine.
- I will not be afraid to showcase my talent.
- I will use my talent to express my greatness.
- I will strive to be great at everything I do.

*N*ow that you See You, it's time to unleash your greatness. Remember to stop looking at yourself as being just ordinary. "You are a Black Girl who has the power to transcend the barriers that are positioned* *to limit you."* God gave you the strength, power, grace, and freedom to live your life in greatness. *Unleash your Greatness!*

Black Girl, we all like to express ourselves in various ways. I love to express who I am through the way I dress, my phone cases, and my hairstyles. How you express yourself tells others how you feel about yourself. Do me a favor and look in the mirror and visualize the person you want to become. Begin to imagine that you are that person. How do you feel? What do you see? What are you doing? How are you acting? How are people responding to you? Begin to express yourself as that person. Romans 4:17 says to "Call those things that are not as though they were." Simply stated, act like you are already the person you desire to become. When you begin to walk in purpose, doors begin to open. Live out loud by expressing you and release your greatness so others can SEE YOU! For example, I want to be a journalist with a law degree and also host my own TV show. When I look in my Mirror of Truth, I grab my hairbrush and pretend to interview people on my show. I also interview myself. Then, I unleash my greatness by dancing to express how I feel so I can begin my day highly motivated to conquer the world.

Your Gifts Will Make Room for You

If you activate your belief in yourself and your purpose, you not only break barriers, but you give power to other Black Girls to do the same. Your gift will always expand. If you fail the first time, get up, adjust your crown, and try again. Winners never quit on themselves!

You don't have to envy another Black Girl's talent. It's okay to use someone else as a guide or admire them. Just remember that your journey is your own. Admiration is great, but just make sure that you aspire to be your authentic self. You don't have to duplicate someone else to get ahead. You are more than talented. You are blessed! Why live your life being fake when real always recognizes real? You are original. Be YOU! Know the truth. Live the truth. It changes everything. *The truth allows you to become relentless so you can unleash your greatness, allowing others to see who you really are.*

I am a strong supporter of those who are not afraid to sing their favorite song when it moves them. Who cares who is listening? It's your way of expressing S.E.L.F., and it can be part of your *IT Flow* regime. So, sing as loud as you can. Dance to your own beat. Express you and watch how you will be able to unleash your greatness. Black girl, you are in for the ride of your life. *Being able to Express You allows you to not be afraid to let your hair down and to let your light shine. Please do not be afraid to show-case your talent, because your boldness will give others permission to showcase theirs.* I am counting on you to express the inner you. Reach deep down into your core and unleash the Black Girl God has called you to become. ***Express yourself in a way that's safe and can heal you.***

Exercise:
List five talents that you have:

1. _____

2. _____

3. _____

4. _____

5. _____

How can you use those talents to express yourself?

_____

_____

_____

_____

_____

_____

_____

_____

_____

_____

_____

_____

_____

Find Your Voice

Finding your voice is not always easy. It takes confidence to trust the voice inside of you to speak for you. It takes more confidence to believe that you have a right to be heard. It is so much easier to be comfortable in the shadows, but remember, you are light. Begin to examine why you shrink back instead of resting in self-confidence.

Have you ever been in class when the teacher asks a question? You know the answer, but no one raises their hands. You don't raise your hand out of fear because, if you are wrong, you don't want your peers to laugh at you. You know the answer and say nothing. The question that you have to ask yourself is: why do I do this? You put in the work. You studied. Why dim your light to resist judgment and make people around you feel comfortable? Why do you hide your intelligence? You must step forward into your intelligence. You have a voice, and you deserve to be heard. You can be assertive and respectful at the same time. Don't shrink back. Stand up, Black Girl! You are *Intelligent & Triumphant*!

I have four ways that will help you to *Unleash Your Greatness.*

1. Discover your Purpose—Jeremiah 29:11

> *"For I know the plans I have for you," declares the LORD, "plans to prosper you and not to harm you, plans to give you hope and a future."*

Complete the following:

1. *What is my purpose on Earth?*

_____

_____

2. *What am I doing now to prepare for my future?*

_____

_____

2. Power—2 Timothy 1:7

> *"For God has not given us a spirit of fear, but of power and of love and of a sound mind."*

Affirm the following:

1. *I have the power and ability to overcome any obstacle that may try to stop me from being a winner.*
2. *I have the power to become whomever I choose.*
3. *I have the power to walk away from negative people and toxic relationships.*
4. *I have the power to say NO!*
5. *I have the power to **Unleash My Greatness.***
6. *I have the power to be Intelligent & Triumphant.*

3. Perseverance—Galatians 6:9

"So let's not get tired of doing what is good. At just the right time we will reap a harvest of blessings if we don't give up."

Complete the following sentence:

1. What are you asking God for?

_____

2. What are you doing now to prepare yourself for your future?

_____

3. What do you want God to bless you with?

_____

4. *How will you use your blessing to help others?*

_____

4. Prosperity—Proverbs 18:16

"A man's gift/talent makes room for him
and brings him before the great."
As you grow, you will prosper and acquire wealth.

Complete the following sentence & affirmations:

1. *My gift/talent is:*

_____

2. *I will pray daily that God will use my gift/talent to inspire others.*

3. *I will strive to perfect my talent so I can create generational wealth.*

4. *I will use my talent to become a multi-millionaire.*

Look in your Mirror of Truth and say:

"Dear S.E.L.F.,
You are Intelligent & Triumphant, and I will
Express You as a Black Girl of Greatness."

Mirror of Truth Reflection:

"Your Journey of Greatness begins when
you open your Soul to Expression."
—Tamera Elyse

Black Girl Prayer for Purpose

Heavenly Father,

Thank you for the gifts and talents that you have placed inside of me. I want to use them to bring glory to you. Teach me how to perfect my gifts. Please begin to show me my purpose. Give me glimpses into my future so that I can begin to prepare for the things that you have for me. Send great teachers and mentors into my life to help guide me on my path. Help me to become comfortable with who I am so that I may be comfortable sharing who I am with the world. I want to become great. I want to live the life that you have prepared for me. Teach me your ways, God. Teach me how to be my true, authentic self.

I love you, God.

Amen.

> **"**
> *"Every word you speak
> to yourS.E.L.F. creates
> your future S.E.L.F."*
>
> ———————————————
>
> TAMERA ELYSE

Chapter Five

Love You

Love the Girl in the Mirror

Mirror of Truth Affirmations:

- I will love me first.
- I will respect myself.
- I will dress with respect.
- I will put my education before boys.
- I will practice abstinence.
- I will not do drugs.

This is the most important chapter because you have to love yourS.E.L.F. before you can love others. I need you to really focus on this chapter. The

Mirror of Truth affirmations are all a result of loving you! To love yourself means you respect yourself first. Loving yourself means you will not allow others to disrespect you or abuse you. Hold yourself to the highest standards of love, honor, and respect. Remember, Black Girl, you are priceless, and your value is far above rubies (Proverbs 31). You are enough!

Now that you See You and you know how to Express You, it is time to LOVE YOU! Remember to stop looking at yourself as just ordinary, but as a Black Girl who has the power to transcend the barriers that are positioned to limit you. God gave you the strength, power, grace, and freedom to live your life in greatness. *Love the girl in the mirror!!!!*

What Is Love?

You may wonder how to love yourself. I know you are told all the time that the best love is S.E.L.F love. This is true. Yet you still may question how to love yourself. Can I be blunt for a moment? Black Girl, S.E.L.F love is not tied into how another human being loves or values you. S.E.L.F love completely comes from inside. It is the love that comes directly from how you feel about yourself. *Every Black Girl is born with the ability to love herself with the purest love that God created.*

The problem is that the image of pure love has been distorted by images of lust, greed, possession, and abuse. The images of Black Girls are so mean and misrepresented. Black Girls are viewed as hateful, ignorant, and full of eye-rolling and head-swinging attitudes. Black Girls are the target of sexual objectification. You can't turn on the television without images of Black Girl bodies displayed for sexual gratification. This is real! What you see and hear about yourself greatly impacts how you view yourself. How can you love yourself when society constantly reminds you that you are not good enough? The images make it seem as though the value of Black Girls lies in wide hips, big butts, small waists, big breasts, and a weave down the back. Come on! Black Girls are so much more than that. In fact, Black Girls aren't that at all. I know it's hard to not get caught up in the hype of it, but you deserve such a better portrait of yourself.

It is hard to replace those images with ones of love in its purest form. You have to retrain your mind to believe that you are capable of loving YOU. The truth of the matter is that there is so much magic within you that you are bursting at the seams with it. You are love!

Remember: *You have to let go of the pain and negative images to see your beauty and intelligence.*

Exercise:

List three negative images about Black Girls that directly impact how you feel about yourself.

1. _____

2. _____

3. _____

Now list five positive images about Black Girls that are the opposite of your negative images.

1. _____

2. _____

3. _____

4. _____

5. _____

Now write down how those positive images can empower you to love yourself daily.

_____

_____

_____

_____

_____

Lets Talk About Sex

Let's get right into it. One of the affirmations says to practice abstinence. You may have moved your head back a bit when you read that, but let me break it down for you. Your value is so awesome and priceless that everyone does not deserve you. As royalty, you have to set the standard of how you are to be treated, cherished, and respected. I'm not telling you to be a Black Girl who feels that she is too good or better than others, but what I am telling you is that you are well within your rights to respect yourself and demand respect from those around you. Remember, people respect what you respect. You must show people how to respect you.

Sex is so intimate. If you have ever listened to the "first-time" stories of the women in your family, I bet you have heard at least one of regret. You are a gift; a precious gift. Wait to give yourself to someone who understands how to adore, cherish, and preserve the gift you are. Save your gift for your husband. Share your gift with the man who makes an outward, vocal commitment through marriage to uphold you. Set the standard. I know you live in a world that tells you to sample everything before you buy it. Here is the truth. Everything doesn't need to be sampled. Just because something is available does not mean that it is good for you or that you need it.

You don't have to wear clothes that show your body to lure someone into liking you. If a boy is coming to you only because he likes what he sees, let him keep walking. He is only coming to conquer what he sees. You are more than your body. You are *Intelligent & Triumphant*. You don't need to sell anything.

On another note, if you have already given away your virginity, don't worry. Just ask God to forgive you, and He will. After you receive God's forgiveness, you can save yourself for your husband. Forgiveness is the gift that God gives to us. Forgive yourself. Also let's be clear, everyone can't pay the cost for you! Your price is above diamonds and rubies. Know that and act accordingly!

Exercise:

What promise are you willing to make to yourself regarding sex, marriage, and your self-worth? This is YOUR promise. Be specific.

Drugs

I hate that we even have to discuss this, because we have all seen what the use and abuse of drugs do to a person. Yet I feel it is necessary because there's a real war out there. Drugs are so easily accessible; they are the most successful word-of-mouth product out here. Bottom line...don't get caught up. Drugs take life from you. You have too much promise within you to be fooled into chasing a high that is not real. You don't want to miss out on life by slowly committing death. There is so much life to be lived. I know, Black Girl, you face so much pressure daily. It can become overwhelming. But, putting a chemical in your body for relief just adds more burden and pressure.

If your life takes a curvy turn that you can't handle, find a confidant. Confide in this person about how you feel and talk about the feelings you are uncertain about. You are not an island. You can't handle pain on your own. Don't isolate yourself. Isolation leaves room for your thoughts to wander. Not all thoughts are good. You have to begin to train yourself in separating the good from the bad. Good thoughts will never tell you to abuse drugs or harm yourself. Hang around other Black Girls who are positive, caring, and uplifting. You never have to resort to drugs. There are more meaningful and purposeful avenues to help you get over the bad and hurtful things happening in your life.

Handle Your Business

Education is the key to success. Let nothing and no one block you from pursuing your dream to graduate college or get educated. My dad always told me that **not everyone will need a degree, but you will need to be educated!** Black Girl, you have the potential and a promise that is important to the future of this world. *Let your intelligence manifest itself so you can be triumphant!*

Don't allow distractions to hinder you from receiving the credentials you need to succeed.

Boys = Distractions.
Friends who aren't really friends = Distractions.
Drugs = Distractions.
Alcohol = Distractions.
Poor choices when you know better = Distractions.

You can't be a BOSS without being educated! Acquire the knowledge so your intelligence can shine! The world is waiting for you! Put your education first, and the rest will fall into place. You are Intelligent & Triumphant. Handle your business!

Exercise:

Write down what you desire to see for yourself in the future. You may not know it all, but that is okay; no one does. However, it is important to have a blueprint. What makes a blueprint great is you can always make changes.

_____

_____

List three universities/trade schools/community colleges you would like to attend.

1. _____

2. _____

3. _____

What is your plan to attend and make one of these universities/trade schools/community colleges a reality?

_____

_____

_____

_____

_____

_____

Loving yourself always starts with how you see yourself, because if you SEE YOU as being *Intelligent & Triumphant*, then your Mirror of Truth affirmations will empower you to love yourself more each day. We all have flaws and imperfections, but so what! YOU ARE FABULOUS without makeup, a weave, or plastic surgery! LOVE the girl in the mirror for who she is and promise yourself that you will love her unconditionally and you will do no harm to her! Learn to love the girl in the mirror regardless of her imperfections.

You are your only limit. There's only one S.E.L.F., so LOVE HER!!!

Look in the mirror and remember to:

- *Love You* despite what others may think about you.
- *Love You* when you fail.
- *Love You* when things don't go your way.
- *Love You* when your parents let you down.
- *Love You* when your best friends turn their backs on you.
- *Love You* when your boyfriend cheats on you.
- *Love You* when your father or mother walks out on you.
- *Love You* whether your hair is short or long.
- *Love You* whether you have light or dark skin.

- *Love You* regardless of your size.
- *Love You* regardless of your social status.

Look in your Mirror of Truth and say:

"Dear S.E.L.F.,
You are Intelligent & Triumphant, and I
Love You as being a Black Girl of Greatness."

Mirror of Truth Reflection:

"Every word you speak to yourS.E.L.F.
creates your future S.E.L.F."
—Tamera Elyse

Black Girl Prayer of Hope

Heavenly Father,

Thank you for hope. Thank you for creating me with potential and purpose and to be a change agent in this world. Thank you for surrounding me with individuals who want only the best for me. Thank you for friends who encourage me. Thank you for my family, who inspire me. Father, I ask that you continue to teach me how to love myself. When the pressure becomes too much or I feel over-whelmed, remind me of your love. Remind me that I am fearfully and wonderfully made. Remind me that you are with me. Help me to not become distracted from walking my journey and reaching my destinations. Remove people from my life who want to cause harm or encourage me to forfeit my dream. I want to become all that you have called me to become.

Love, the Black Girl with Hope.

Amen.

> "When you know who you are and where you belong, only then can you walk in Truth & Freedom."

TAMERA ELYSE

Chapter Six

Free You

Dance to Your Own Rhythm

Mirror of Truth Affirmations:

- I will live and not die.
- I am my Sister's Keeper.
- I will be kind to others.
- I will rise above being petty.
- I will encourage others.
- I will not speak negativity to myself or others.
- I will create my own rhythm to dance to.
- I will dance daily.
- I will dance in truth, love, and encouragement.

No Excuses. Be *Intelligent & Triumphant*

Now that you have established how to *S*ee You, *E*xpress You, and *L*ove You, it's time to *F*ree You. This is the moment of truth. This is where you get to free the person you have become and are destined to be in the future. The person you have become will have a great impact on others, so be careful as to who and what you allow in your daily IT Flow. This is the moment you dance to your own rhythm. This is the moment you give permission to the Black Girl in the mirror to be free. *"Free yourself from negative friends, toxic relationships, negative thoughts about yourself, and anyone who does not appreciate you!"*

You will no longer speak negative about yourself. You recognize how toxic negative talk can be and how it can stunt your growth. Listen, every day will not be wonderful. That's life. However, your bounce-back has to be just as stable, secure, and real as your come-up. Real talk, real growth happens during the bounce-back. Life is crazy. You know this. Yet you have to make up your mind that you won't be defeated by life. You shall live and not die! You have one shot at this…so shoot your shot, Black Girl, and live life!!!

Black Girl Journal Entry:

Write down what you are freeing yourself from. It can be thoughts, people, places, etc. Why did they have you bound? What is giving you the courage to set yourself free?

_____

_____

_____

_____

_____

_____

_____

_____

_____

_____

_____

_____

_____

_____

_____

_____

_____

Free You to dream big like our pioneers so you can make history, Black Girl, **You can do it. I believe in you!** Use your *IT Flow* and create your own rhythm for your life. Pass on your *IT Flow* to other Black Girls. Show them how to get their own *IT Flow*. Be the one who straightens another Black Girl's crown without telling the world it was crooked. *Inspire. Empower. Motivate. Support.* Your light will never grow dim by helping another Black Girl into the spotlight. There is room for everyone. In fact, *when we support one another in love, we send a message to the world that we are love and there is a positive movement in numbers. Encourage not only through your actions, but with your words. Speak life. Speak hope. Speak change.*

Exercise:
List five ways that you can support other Black Girls in their journey to success.

1. _____

2. _____

3. _____

4. _____

5. _____

Black Girl, you have to feed your *S.E.L.F.* daily with the food from my Winner's Recipe, which is to *Speak IT, Believe IT, Live IT, and Work IT!* This is what the IT Flow Movement is all about. Use your intelligence and become what God has called you to be. Black Girl, you just need to believe that you are *Intelligent & Triumphant.* *"So as a woman thinketh in her heart, so is she" (Proverbs 23:7).*

Exercise:
SPEAK IT:
What do you SPEAK to yourself now?

_____

_____

_____

_____

_____

_____

_____

BELIEVE IT:
What do you BELIEVE about yourS.E.L.F. now?

_____

_____

_____

_____

_____

_____

_____

_____

LIVE IT:
How do you intend to live the new YOU in your daily life?

_____

_____

_____

_____

_____

_____

_____

WORK IT:
How do you plan to WORK it, Black Girl?

_____

_____

_____

_____

_____

_____

_____

I believe in you, and I pray that the Black Girl you discover in your Mirror of Truth will blossom into a future *S.E.L.F.* with unlimited opportunities. I pray that you will create your own rhythm and dance to it daily so you can unleash your greatness and the world can see who you really are! ***Black Girl, feel your heartbeat and celebrate who you have become.***

Dear Black Girl, You are Intelligent & Triumphant, and I am so proud of YOU!

Once again, thank you for joining me on my *IT Flow Movement.* ***Don't forget to show others how to create their own rhythm so they can dance for life!***

Look in your Mirror of Truth and say:

"Dear S.E.L.F.,
You are Intelligent & Triumphant, and I Free
You to become a Black Girl of Greatness."

Mirror of Truth Reflection:

"When you know who you are and where you belong, only then can you walk in Truth & Freedom."
—Tamera Elyse

Black Girl Prayer of Freedom

Heavenly Father,

Thank you for loving me enough to show me how to use my Intelligence to manifest my gifts so that I can be Triumphant in every area of my life. Remove any fears, obstacles or barriers that may try to hinder me from living on purpose. Thank you for the freedom I have found within myself. Thank you for allowing me to Love the Black Girl in the Mirror. Thank you for showing me how to See myself, Express myself, Love myself and to Free myself. Father, please continue to show me how to be Intelligent & Triumphant so that I can live a free lifestyle of winning. I know that sometimes, I may fail, but I know that I am more than a conqueror, and I can get back up and continue to win. Thank you for helping me to see my inner beauty regardless of my flaws and imperfections. Thank you for creating me in your image and thank you for the New Black Girl, I am destined to become, as of today.

I Love You, God.

Amen.